BlockChain

Learn Block Chain Technology Quickly

What you need to know in an hour

By

Daniel Reed

Table of Contents

Introduction

I want to thank you and congratulate you for purchasing this book, *"Block Chain - Learn Blockchain Technology Quickly*. What you need to know in an hour"*.

This book contains proven steps and strategies on how you can make use of the blockchain technology. Within this book are all the details that you need to fully grasp how blockchain works and how you can mine bitcoins or ether by being part of a blockchain network.

The blockchain is the revolutionary technology that is believed to change the way people do transactions online. By learning how this technology works and how you can use it, you will be able to take part of one of the biggest innovation today and get an insight on how the world's future online transactions will be.

I hope you enjoy it!

Chapter 1

What is Blockchain?

A blockchain, on a surface level, functions like the Google spreadsheet that you may use on a regular basis – people can write on it, and you can keep track of all the changes that are made among the users who has the permission to edit it. You may think of your spreadsheet as a very important tool that keeps all your data in check and can be updated on a regular basis.

Today, most of the transactions that you do daily is stored on a company's database – your online purchases, social media entries, blog uploads, etc. needs to be kept in a secure server so that you can keep track of what's happening to them. However, you know that the world is not a perfect place. It is always possible for a server to go down, crippling thousands or even millions of online consumers that will not be able to access a data or service that they need. It is also possible for irregularities to happen in-between transaction. That makes every consumer want a system that they can easily check and would be secure enough for all their transactions to never be tampered with for anyone's gain.

The blockchain technology promises to do all that by keeping a decentralized ledger of transactions, that allows everyone access for the right checks and balances. When implemented across industries, this technology will change the way you think about security and transparency.

The Database that Everyone Will Love

The blockchain technology is essentially a piece of software that aims to consolidate data into a one big chain of events. Its aim is to make sure that data is stored in a chronological manner and that there is no way for transactions that are stored in it become changed. It also makes it a point that everyone can see the flow of transaction. Compared to normal ledgers, you cannot make erasures on this ledger – once a piece of information is already confirmed, it cannot be taken out anymore.

You can think of the blockchain as a Lego set that is made of data. Within a box set, you could get different pieces and then connect them together and they will fit perfectly. However, you would want to create a certain design, so you would want to fit the blocks together in a certain manner. However, once you put the pieces together, it would be impossible for anyone to take them apart – you can only add to the chain of blocks that you have already created, but you cannot take out a piece.

Think of the usual database – when you do one transaction after the other, you expect them to follow an order so you can easily validate if all the information is there. However, databases that people usually use can be easily changed or even lost – they are either stored in a facility that can easily be accessed, or someone working from the inside of the facility can steal or tamper with them. Now, what if everyone that has a computer can have access to those databases? Everyone will easily find out if something is changed in someone's copy because their own copy of the data will tell so. Also, everyone should agree whether a certain addition to the database is acceptable or not, based on rules that everybody agrees on.

By decentralizing data, or making everyone privy to information, you can trust that there is no one out there that will singlehandedly destroy data or make unwanted changes on it, thus making the distributed information very secure. Also, by having a system that tells whether a certain set of data is valid or not, the system is not likely to be rigged by an individual.

What makes it even better is that it can to accept transactions from numerous parties, as long as they are involved in the chain of transactions. It doesn't matter where you are in the world – if you do a transaction that belongs to a certain chain, then your data can be stored securely in this electronic ledger. Compared to most databases that exist today, you can include your information in a blockchain without having to sign up for a third party's service.

To sum it up, blockchains are the solution that everybody needs to prevent data manipulation, and there are a lot of benefits that will stem from that. By solving the issue of data manipulation, everyone can enjoy a more transparent and accessible data management without having to rely on any third party to do that job. What people can expect soon are transactions that are faster and more secure.

Do Blockchains Exist Now?

Yes, there are blockchains that are fully functional right now. One of the most popular blockchains is the bitcoin, which is a cryptocurrency that can be used to buy goods and avail services. Since the bitcoin is maintained by a blockchain, you can actually see all the transactions that involves a bitcoin, which includes the transaction done in order to produce the first bitcoin, and how people send money to others. When you go to www.blockchain.info, you can actually see a graphical interface that shows you the entire chain of transactions done using this currency.

There is also a blockchain that is dedicated making decentralized applications, which means that there are people that are starting to make some services available to people without a single company owning managing the use. This means that when successful, the applications that they are creating will never suffer from outages, making them more stable than programs that run on private servers.

There are also blockchains owned by private organizations that are created to make their own private database secure by taking advantage of the tamper-proof quality of data storage that the blockchain offers.

The blockchain technology is also starting to get rolled out on many banks and legal firms, essentially to maintain the integrity of their records and confirm transactions faster than they used to be.

Blockchains Will Free the Way People Transact

Blockchains are created in such a way that it would change the way people create transactions and trust services that they want to avail. It is designed in a manner that solves most of the people's issues when it comes to creating transactions with virtually everyone in the world, no matter where they are. By making this technology possible, everyone can have the freedom that they want to enjoy when they make exchanges and use platforms that are available to them.

Blockchains are thought to impact world's processes more than what the internet did to the postal service. It is bound to change almost everything that you can do that involves internet connectivity and is predicted to affect everyone who uses smart devices and computers. Its functions are also thought to affect everyone that accesses and processes data with a massive chain effect to the point that it will disrupt every industry that involved the use of data.

Chapter 2

How Blockchain Works

You can think of the blockchain as a very large spreadsheet available on your Google Drive. However, changing even a single entry on that spreadsheet would require a very special permission: it cannot be edited unless everybody that has access to that spreadsheet agrees to the changes that are proposed to be made. However, the only change that they can do to it is to add additional data, which will still be approved by everyone that is within the group.

What is the Blockchain Supposed to Do

At this point, you know that blockchain is essentially a software that is designed to work like a shareable Excel spreadsheet, only that it is more secure.

All transactions that make use of the blockchain are guaranteed safe, because a blockchain does not rely on any third party to run or maintain its ledger, it relies on a blockchain network. This network makes use of a protocol based on consensus, which means that the majority of those that belong to that network needs to agree that the contents that are going to be added to it are legitimate. Furthermore, those that belong to the blockchain network makes it a point that all transactions are secured by using hashes and the transaction owner's digital signatures.

Consensus is achieved because everybody in the network has the exact copy of the transaction. This means that if there is anyone that wants to tamper with a single transaction will have to find a way to make changes to all copies that are spread all throughout the world. What makes security in a blockchain even better is that all those transactions that are added into the blockchain are hashed using the SHA256. The SHA 256 is an algorithm that is designed to create a one-way encryption. Once a transaction is encrypted, there is virtually no way for one to decrypt it back to its original form. For this reason, no one in the network really knows what the transaction that they are trying to validate really is from, making all transactions anonymous.

Ensuring Legitimate Transactions

If all transactions in the blockchain are anonymous, how does one make sure that they are done by a legitimate person that is capable of holding their end of the bargain? This is solved by enforcing the use of the digital signature, which ensures that all people that are doing exchanges within the blockchain are legitimate users and not mere imposters.

At the same time, digital signatures also add another layer of security by making use of private keys in a very public ledger. While all things that are happening within the blockchain community are already secured by their hashes, people also need privacy. You can just imagine what will happen if everybody knows that you have a certain amount of bitcoins (which, today, is a lucrative currency to have). By also encrypting information about transaction owners, everybody will have the peace of mind about their personal data.

Chapter 3

Difference Between Blockchain and Bitcoin

You have probably heard about bitcoins if you are reading this. Or someone might have mentioned about it and you became curious.

What is a Bitcoin?

The bitcoin is a cryptocurrency that was introduced in 2008. During that time, Occupy Wall Street made strong statements against the alleged manipulation of giant financial corporations of the economy – misappropriation of funds, outright fraud, overcharging, you name it. In an essence, the bitcoin currency is introduced as an attempt to solve all problems that a centralized form of money management has – it aims to get rid of the consumer's need for an intermediary, the need to pay for transaction fees, and to make sure that all transactions that involve money are transparent. The bitcoin has created a decentralized economic system wherein consumers can freely choose who to send their money to and know what exactly takes place when they store or spend it.

The bitcoin has grown exponentially since the time of its introduction. It used to be only used in underground transactions, but now, almost every industry makes use of it. You can even include fintech giants such as Visa, Mastercard, and PayPal among its users.

A Closer Look at Bitcoin

Bitcoin, just like every currency out there that you can use, can be used for exchanges because it has an ascribed value. The only difference it has from fiat money is that it is a virtual currency – it is not represented by anything tangible, but the technology enables you to use it for exchanges. As a form of cryptocurrency, you can use this to buy goods or avail services.

If you have a bitcoin and you make transactions, the blockchain network will send the person who will be receiving your funds an encrypted code, which will contain the necessary information that will verify your identity. It will also tell the other party that you have enough funds to cover the transaction. The other party will decrypt the transaction's code using a program and will then receive your bitcoins.

Is the Blockchain the Bitcoin?

The bitcoin makes use of the blockchain technology, but no, they are not the same. The bitcoin does possess the qualities of the blockchain, which are the following:

• Irreversible

Once a transaction using bitcoin is confirmed, there is no way for this to be reversed. Since it works on a decentralized structure, there is no one out there that can help you cancel or make changes to your transaction.

• Pseudonymous

Bitcoin transactions are never connected to real-world personalities – there is no one in the world that will know how you are spending or receiving bitcoins over the network. To receive bitcoins, you send people a public bitcoin wallet address so they will know where to send the cryptocurrency. However, that public address is different from your private key, which adds another layer of security to your private details.

Because all transactions are hashed on the blockchain network, you can only analyze the flow of transactions in a blockchain network. However, it is impossible for you to connect a person to a bitcoin wallet, especially if you are looking at the entire bitcoin ledger online.

• Fast and far-reaching

If you do any transaction over a bitcoin network, you can expect your transaction to be processed within minutes. That's right – you do not wait for hours to send or receive payments, compared to traditional payment systems that you use which make use of third party processors. What's more is that the bitcoin network is indifferent to location – sending money to a person that lives in another continent is just as fast as sending funds to a person next door.

• Secure

Just like all other transactions that make use of the blockchain technology, a bitcoin transaction is encrypted with a one-way hash, which is virtually impossible to decrypt. This makes all transactions done using a bitcoin tamper-proof.

• Permission-less

The software that you can use to do transactions using a bitcoin is free – that means that the application that you can use is not developed by a third party that will charge you for transactions or tell you whether you can send money or not to a different person. No one can prevent you from transacting with anyone using your bitcoins.

Mining Bitcoins

If you want to start getting your hands on some bitcoins and you want to buy them, then you have probably heard about bitcoin mining. Bitcoin mining is essentially the way people controlling nodes, or computers that are participating in verifying bitcoin transactions, create new bitcoins for the network by confirming transactions in the blockchain network.

This means that by mining, transactions within a blockchain network are secured and locked into blocks. This is done by solving the nonce (also known as number used only once), which is based on a cryptographic problem that is based on the SHA 256 algorithm. This compensates those who are spending resources to confirm transactions and to generate new bitcoins to spread around.

Chapter 4

Benefits of Using Blockchain

While the blockchain is extremely popular in running cryptocurrencies such as bitcoin, this technology can interrupt the way several industries operate. Because blockchain is designed to free several industries from a lot of limitations, this revolutionary technology might just replace many organizations that you are so used to dealing with daily.

Introduction of the Trustless Exchange

One of the main goals of the blockchain is to create a world where there is no middleman. This greatly reduces third-party risks.

More Efficient Transactions

Once this technology is adopted by several industries, transactions can be done faster because they do not have to be confirmed by any centralized organization. Transactions done over the blockchain network experience less risk of not being confirmed or processed since they are not likely to experience downtime, compared to transactions that are needed to be stored or process. Since consumers don't have to avail a centralized party's services for their transactions to push through, they also avoid high transaction fees.

Empowered Users

Without having to conform to the rules of intermediaries that approve transactions, everybody will have the freedom of controlling their transactions. At the same time, people will also have the ability to monitor all activities that concern their transactions.

Data Security and Reliability

Decentralized networks that process and store data makes all transactions secure – since the blockchain does not rely on a single physical network to process and store user information, it is not likely to come to a halt and delete information that it already contains. Within the same vein, blockchains are also virtually impregnable – it would be impossible for anyone to decrypt its one-way hash or attack all the computers that are storing blockchain data, which makes it more capable of withstanding attacks.

Integrity of Processes

Once a blockchain is designed to perform tasks in a certain way, there is no way for someone to change its protocols. Because of this, you can always be certain that transactions do not skip a process or become altered while being confirmed.

Simplified Ecosystems

Because all transactions that are done within a blockchain are stored in a single ledger that everybody can view, organizations that use it does not have to deal with having to create multiple ledgers or databases. Everybody can rely on a published ledger in order to keep track of data.

Chapter 5

Disadvantages of Using the Blockchain

The blockchain technology is a work in progress. At this point, several technologies are still being developed to make sure that it does what it needs to do, which is to make its users perform transactions without the risk of their data being compromised. Despite all the promises that the blockchain aims to deliver, no one can say that it is perfect.

To some, blockchain exists as the utopia for financial technology and other industries that it aims to changes. However, there are still plenty of challenges to be addressed.

Shaky Regulatory Status

If you are thinking of investing in cryptocurrency, making sure of its legality in your region is necessary. Right now, there are certain areas that prohibit the use of the bitcoin for exchanges. Because the blockchain is still a technology that is still under development, there is a possibility of dispute about existing regulations on how transactions will be processed and how this technology may replace existing processes that still work for the consumers.

The Challenge of the Network Size

While the blockchain is created to withstand attacks, being impregnable would depend on the size of its network. That means that if this technology will not gain the participation of computers in a variety of locations across the globe, then it becomes possible for attackers to find out where the nodes or computers that are confirming the transactions are. While it is easier to penetrate centralized servers, a network that is too small is still very possible to attack.

Speed and Cost

Having a decentralized mode of storing and processing data may seem to be ideal, if the system is already matured. However, blockchain networks are still relatively new and the nodes that are working to confirm transactions may not be enough to process all transactions that happen in a day. As of this writing, combined networks working for the bitcoin blockchain can confirm 243,623 transactions within 24 hours. Visa, one of the fintech giants in the world, can confirm 150,000,000 transactions every day. Looking at this numbers, it looks like the bitcoin blockchain needs a lot of work when it comes to improving transaction speed.

At the same time, now is not yet the time when bitcoin transactions are affordable for the middle-class consumer. Bitcoin transactions become more expensive, depending on the amount of storage space they occupy, and the current norm is that transactions that have higher transaction fees get prioritized. The average transaction fee, as of this writing, would cost around $2.45. However, transactions that have this fee usually gets confirmed after an hour or a day.

Risk of Human Error

If you are going to use a database that doesn't easily allow you to make changes, then you need to make sure that all the entries that go there are of high quality. While there is nothing you can do to alter the contents of the transactions (which gives you the idea that the system is secure), you need to have all the checks and balances to ensure that all entries that enter the ledger are accurate.

Mining Consumption

There is a reason people get paid for solving the cryptographic puzzle to confirm transactions – mining bitcoins and confirming blocks can be costly. Combining the electricity consumption and hardware costs can be too much for an ordinary PC owner. While the logic for the requirement for miners to have Proof of Work is to make sure that making changes to a transaction is as difficult as adding a transaction to a block, miners are also doing the same task to solve the nonce first, which does not really make the confirming network very efficient.

For this reason, many blockchain developers are switching the method that their coins can be mined and how transactions can be validated. Certain blockchains, such as the Ethereum and the Peercoin are making the big switch from Proof of Work to a greener and more viable way of making their nodes work to confirm blocks.

Scalability Issues

At this point, the blockchain being used by bitcoin can push for seven transaction confirmations per second. However, there are doubts if all blockchains will be able to have a capacity to confirm more transactions. At this point, the blockchain has a peak capacity of 56,000 transactions per second, but for the amount of transactions that needs to be confirmed across the globe, it still needs to scale to accommodate more and enhance blockchain services.

Blockchains aim to resolve this by encouraging more people to join their network to confirm transactions by incentivizing participation. With the hopes of getting more nodes to participate in validating transactions and making changes on the way they can be confirmed, more developed blockchains are aiming to solve this issue in the very near future.

The Possibility of the 51% Attack

The blockchain network confirms that a transaction should push through based on consensus. This means that at least 51% of the confirming computers should agree that a transaction is valid before it pushes through. This way, people can trust that the blockchain is secure in such a way that there is no single point of vulnerability that could collapse its entire structure.

However, there is the possibility of the 51% attack, or a possible "rigging" of results by a more dominant sector of the confirming network. Those that are in favor of the blockchain think that this type of attack is not close to reality, but there are cyber security experts, such as Kaspersky, that argue that this is still likely to happen given the norms of mining nowadays.

Proof of Work, which is essentially having to spend electricity, hardware, and time for a computer to guess the cryptographic puzzle needed to confirm a block (and earn bitcoins in the process), is the reason blocks of information get attached to a blockchain. However, what miners aim to do nowadays is not to confirm transactions but to hoard the bitcoin. When this happens, the bitcoin is not distributed across the worldwide grid – those that are able to afford spending for energy consumption and the rig will end up controlling the bitcoin mining game. When you think about it, there are numerous fintech giants that can readily avail the machinery for mining. Visa, for example, is upping their game by investing in hardware and consumption that will allow them to confirm transactions in seconds. To date, China is the country that is leading in producing and using bitcoin mining rigs. With mining nodes concentrated to certain countries or corporations, rigging the mining game for a 51% attack becomes a huge possibility.

Because this flaw has already been predicted, several alternative blockchains and their cryptocurrencies are making some changes on how transactions can be verified and how their currencies can be spread along their grids.

Would Blockchain Evolve to Defeat Challenges?

The blockchains that you know now are probably not the blockchains that you will be using in the future. The bitcoin blockchain, for example, is still at an incredibly young age – it is rough around the edges, but it shows where improvements should happen. Being able to understand how the blockchain can improve will allow this technology to be the promising data structure that people want it to be.

Chapter 6

The Blockchain and the Finance Industry

The financial system across the globe works to serve billions of people in a day, and moves large sums of currency in the process. However, the traditional financial setting faces numerous challenges, which include arduous paperwork, document mismatch, exorbitant transaction fees, plus numerous opportunities for fraud.

While the current financial system seems to work on the surface, Pricewaterhouse Coopers (PWC) reported that about half of today's intermediaries that serve the financial sector suffers economic crime annually. That means that all the institutions that you currently trust to secure and process your financial records and transactions, which include money transfer third parties, payment services, and even stock exchanges, are compromised one way or another. The current solution for intermediaries to continue providing trust is to increase regulatory costs, which is of course transferred to consumers like you.

The financial system makes use of processes and technologies that may be antiquated – when everything fails, people will be forced to go back to paper-based transactions that are vulnerable to error and manipulation. At the same time, it is also centralized, which makes it vulnerable to system attacks or technical difficulties, which brings back the consumer to the hassle of the first scenario. Also, it is extremely exclusionary – it essentially denies billions of consumers the very tools that they need to ensure that transparency is in place. The proposed solution for all these, as you may have already thought of, is the blockchain.

The Best Way to Do Exchanges

You already know that blockchain can give birth to cryptocurrency, such as the bitcoin, but that is only a small part of what this technology can do. With blockchain, it is possible for you to do asset exchange in a secure manner, thanks to cryptography, the digital signature, and network consensus. On top of that, it enables two individuals to make an agreement and do an exchange without knowing each other, but still trust that they are dealing with a legitimate entity that can hold their end of the bargain. All these are done without having to rely on a middleman to verify identities and permit the transaction to happen.

What Will Happen to the Banking System?

Right now, banks are the ones that are going to be disrupted the most by this technology if they do not do the necessary upgrades. For this reason, many financial giants are starting to invest in blockchain solutions, which provides them the benefit of reducing cost and friction with intermediaries that they also use. Because banks can easily process transactions on their own without having to rely on third party solutions, the use of blockchain may lower the cost of banking. While they are not keen on replacing the fiat currency with cryptocurrency, the banking system can definitely benefit from what this system has to offer.

Known intermediaries, such as Visa and Mastercard, are also jumping in into the blockchain investment as well. In the future, you may expect more fintech giants promoting services that make use of this ledger system.

Most experts say that genuine disruption of the blockchain to the finance industry is yet to happen in a decade. You could probably imagine financial transactions that are free from data manipulation, human error, and high cost would happen within seconds. Right now, the fintech side of the blockchain is still under development; however, the above promises are the things that you can count on.

Chapter 7

Blockchain and Other Industries

While financial services are the first ones to employ the blockchain system, other industries are also bound to improve when they use this technology. Even without having to delve with cryptocurrency, other industries will also benefit from incorporating blockchain into their processes.

Healthcare

Digital signatures that are present in data stored in blockchains will promote the privacy and availability of health records. At the same time, using blockchains and ensuring that medical facilities, insurance companies, and health practitioners are part of the blockchain will drastically reduce instances of fraud in this industry.

Government

Government offices can definitely benefit from blockchain when it comes to expediting exchange of information between departments, which is bound to improve government services. Through blockchain, government offices can also make sure that data is released in real time in order for certain policies to be enforced in a timely manner. This will greatly affect government actions that are time-sensitive, such as emergency responses.

Blockchain will also impact fact-checking because it will make a more transparent means for citizens to access government transactions and fund allocation. In its very nature, blockchain will combat corruption across government offices and push for transparency in public documents and available services.

Law

Blockchains prove to be capable of storing huge amounts of information, which will include contracts. Smart contracts, or protocols that make sure that what is stated in the contract is the only action allowed in a particular blockchain, will affect how contracts that are already agreed upon by two parties can be fulfilled. Because smart contracts will force agreements to be met, no one will have need a law practitioner to act as a middleman. For example, you would not need a legal firm to ensure that you are going to be paid a certain amount when you submit a project to a client.

Energy Industry

The power generation business can benefit from the blockchain's ability to register alternative means to generation. By employing a smart contract, people will be able to find a way to get credits for alternative energy that they will be able to provide.

It's a good thing that energy producers and consumers have already found a way for them to directly transact with each other, without having to rely on giant third parties that will tell them where they can get their energy from. Right now, the startup TransactiveGrid started using the Ethereum (you will know more about this later) in order to make it possible for producers and consumers to transact directly in a peer-to-peer manner

Crowdfunding

Right now, crowdfunding relies on intermediaries, such as Kickstarter and Gofundme, in order to have platforms where they can raise funds for projects or startups. While the known platforms make it possible to enforce trust between project makers and their supporters, they do cut a huge percent of the funds that are going to be raised.

This scenario will change once blockchain enters this industry – project creators will be able to find a way to provide tokens as rewards to their backers, which they can exchange for goods or services at a later time.

Online Media

If you are an independent artist and you want to come up with a way to get payment directly from your listeners, then blockchain is your friend. Blockchain will enable you to sell and license your music without having to rely on platforms such as Spotify, which will take a cut from your earnings. At the same time, blockchains also provide a more efficient cataloging system for those that produce and distribute online music, which makes it easier for fans to discover you.

Just like in the music industry, all other types of media will benefit from the low costs of transactions, which means that applications in the media industry can process transactions without having to pay fees. It also broadens up the options that consumers can enjoy when trying to access media online. For example, a website that runs a magazine can start charging their readers on a per-article basis, instead of having to lock them for an entire month.

Voting

Blockchain offers a smart solution to prevent fraud in voting, thanks to its efficient identity verification and smart contracts which will ensure that only legitimate entries are counted for polls. Of course, once a vote enters the system, it cannot be changed or removed without having to disrupt the entire network of computers that operate it.

Communications and the IoT

One of the biggest strengths of the blockchain technology is to support anything that exists on the internet that involves transactions. This will drastically improve coordination in the Internet of Things (IoT), which will allow multiple devices to coordinate more seamlessly.

Hospitality and Travel

Businesses that cater to consumers by offering travel and hospitality services can enjoy a much-simplified system of settlements. At the same time, blockchains can even support loyalty points systems that most businesses in this industry offer – it can speed up the process of points verification and offer rewards without delay.

Credit and Reputation

By having a distributed database that caters to reviews, people and businesses can enjoy trustworthy endorsements without having to rely on third parties to do the survey for them.

The Supply Chain

Consumers can enjoy better transparency on how the products they consume are created with a decentralized system that will display all transactions that transpire from the manufacturer or farm to their households. When the blockchain is widely-adopted by different consumer markets, you will no longer have to be concerned about the origins of the products that you purchase – all you would need to do is check the database for verification.

Your Industry

If your industry needs to store data and requires security and transparency, then it can definitely benefit from implementing the blockchain technology. Blockchains will also offer you the opportunity to speed up certain processes that you may be implementing right now, thanks to decentralization. In the future, you may expect most of the businesses and organizations that you are transacting with to be adopting a system that closely resembles a blockchain, or fully adapt this technology.

Chapter 8

Ethereum and Other Cryptocurrencies

Bitcoin might be the trendsetter when it comes to cryptocurrencies, but it is not the only cryptocurrency out there. As of this writing, there are more than 900 virtual currencies that exist and are actually being mined and used for exchanges all over the world. You can expect this number to grow over time.

Cryptocurrencies, such as the Bitcoin, can be created by anyone that has the ability to mine and sell them to the public to be used for exchanges. Just like fiat money, such as the dollar, these virtual currencies have value that goes up and down depending on their scarcity and utility.

Of course, it is also important to remember that cryptocurrencies are designed to power the blockchain that they are running in. Knowing them equates to knowing what kind of blockchain they serve and what this blockchain aims to achieve in its creation. Within this chapter, you will learn how blockchains could transcend the goal of merely replacing the fiat currency when doing financial transactions, but also change different industries that are still running on the traditional and centralized structures.

What other cryptocurrencies are making it big in the market right now? Here are the virtual currencies that are making waves across industries.

Peercoin

Peercoin's goal is to become secure and decentralized without making its blockchain's network spend a lot in order to make it grow. Its distinguishable feature is that it provides an annual incentive for those who have it, and that it is not very strict on the number of coins that will be available on the market.

This cryptocurrency is thought to be the solution for possible sustainability for the cryptocurrency. While it is currently being mined using the Proof of Work system, it is making a transition to Proof of Stake, which is a system that will make way for new coins on the system without having to invest too much on energy consumption.

Current price: 1 PPC = 1.23

Market cap: $29,862,334

Nxt

Nxt advertises itself as one of the second-generation cryptocurrencies, which means that this cryptocurrencydoes not concern itself with having to function as one of the standalone currencies out there, but to provide a true decentralized platform for exchanges that are happening online. The creators of this currency don't focus on just hitting the goal of becoming a large currency, but to actually create a sound economic ecosystem online. For this reason, people may recognize the Nxt as a platform for online exchanges or a marketplace rather than an actual currency.

One of the great features of Nxt is that it offers its users the option to "shuffle" their coins, which means that those who are exchanging using Nxt coins have a way to obscure their transactions and gain anonymity.

Current price: I NXT = $0.062792

Market cap: $62,729,604

Namecoin

Namecoin is one of the revolutionary cryptocurrencies out there that goes beyond being involved in mere financial transactions. Being one of the early alternative cryptocurrencies out there, this cryptocurrency is powering a P2P technology for verification that makes it possible for people to create websites that are not reliant on popular servers.

Compared to most of the cryptocurrencies out there, the Namecoin is not designed to increase its price – it is actually programmed to make people enjoy lower transaction fees when they try to get a domain for them to join a decentralized internet. This allows future webmasters to enjoy a blockchain that is designed to make it easier for them to create websites without the high cost of acquiring domain names and getting their content on a server.

Current price: 1 NMC = $1.24

Market cap: $18,326,482

Factom

Factom is one of the cryptocurrencies that enjoy a huge market. Known for using a blockchain that is designed to create immutable databases for corporations, the blockchain behind it is designed to create a database that is stored in the Factom blockchain, which is then hashed and stored into the Bitcoin blockchain. Right now, the people behind Factom are working on also adding the Factom hash into other large blockchains for an extra layer of protection to their users.

Factom's current clients include China's smart cities. For a continually growing currency, it is making quite a smart move to offer their technology to governments for streamlined services and data security.

Current Price: 1 FCT = $19.98851064

Market Cap: $174,801,564.3

Litecoin

Litecoin is dubbed as the "silver to the Bitcoin's gold". What makes it special is that it is widely used by independent contractors and that it involves a script (aptly called scrypt) that makes mining impartial to those that have more advanced mining hardware. This cryptocurrency is widely accepted by developers, but the number of merchants that accept this is also growing in number, making it one of the virtual currencies that is worth investing in

Current price: 1 LTC = $ 48.0946294

Market Cap: $2.54 billion

Zcash

Zcash was one of the younger cryptocurrency that has a lot of promise. Zcash defines itself as the https of the Bitcoins http and boasts of better privacy and selective transparency among its users. In Zcash, all transactions are still recorded on the blockchain, but it keeps more sensitive information such as the amount, sender, and recipient more private. What makes it even better is that users that make use of this cryptocurrency has the option to make transactions that are "shielded", which allows users to make use of the zero-knowledge proof (ZPK).

Current price: 1 ZEC = $172.859861

Market Cap: $ 268.91 million

Dash

Formerly known as the Darkcoin, this cryptocurrency is considered to be the most anonymous currency – while it works on a decentralized network like other currencies, it also runs on a mastercode network which makes transactions very hard to trace.

Current price: 1 Dash = $250.144451

Market cap: $1.89 billion

Ripple

This cryptocurrency boasts of instant, sure, and cheap international payments, which makes it a great alternative to current money-sending options. It has a ledger that does not make use of mining, which makes it very different from most cryptocurrencies out there. Since this currency does not need to be mined, it drastically reduces the network's need to use electricity and ensures that the confirming network experiences less latency. Instead, Ripple works to provide incentives to those nodes for their behavior. Ripple targets to distribute the currency to those businesses that need to make up for tighter payment spreads.

Current price: 1 XRP = $0.1817744

Market cap: $6.96 billion

Monero

If you are gunning for an untraceable, and ultimately private and secure, currency, then Monero will be something that you will be interested in. This cryptocurrency grew out of community participations and is donation-based and has a strong focus on growth and decentralization. Its blockchain works with the use of the ring signature, which is designed to shroud the real participant among a "ring" of signatures – since all the cryptographic signatures are designed to appear valid, it would be hard to trace which is the real one.

Current price: 1 XMR = $ 98.7014872

Market cap: $1.4 billion

Ethereum

The Ethereum is one of the cryptocurrencies that are growing fast, and according to Coinbase.com, it is the forefront of the cryptocurrency. The reason is simple – the blockchain behind it is designed not just to secure transactions, but to allow freedom in creating possibilities through apps.

The Ethereum is designed by scripting languages that are, compared to the Bitcoin, very unrestrictive. Instead on focusing on transfers and securing exchanges, the Ethereum introduces the bleeding edge of cryptocurrencies by welcoming the developer community to create decentralized apps, or dapps, which are designed to follow their design. What makes the Ethereum blockchain extremely functional in decentralizing exchanges is that it is dedicated to creating applications that will allow more possibilities online, making transactions that you probably never thought of to be possible. The secret sauce behind it is the development of applications that actually doesn't need any third party to run, which makes a lot of sense in the very goal that the blockchain technology aims to achieve.

Current price: 1 ETH = $256.019334

Market cap: $24.22 billion

Introducing the Proof of Stake

While the Bitcoin is mined through Proof of Work, the Ethereum will eventually grow and get scattered around the globe through Proof of Stake. While both types of transaction validation aim to achieve a distributed consensus among the network, The Proof of Stake determines who will create the new block on the blockchain in a mode deterministic manner – those that have already participated in the Ethereum blockchain gets chosen, and that chosen one does not get a reward.

What makes the Proof of Stake an awesome way of validating transactions? Proof of Work is not necessarily an environmentally-healthy way of mining for cryptocurrency. Mining for a block on the Bitcoin blockchain takes a lot of energy. How much energy is that? One transaction requires the amount of electricity that could power almost 2 American households. A block is a group of transactions, and that is a lot of energy consumption in total. This is not just unhealthy for the environment, but could be unhealthy for the economy as well since electricity is being paid for by fiat currency.

Under the Proof of Stake mining system, people are compensated by transaction fees instead of a substantial reward. Participants that want to validate transactions are those that actually have an Ether, while the Proof of Work system makes anyone with the ample computing hardware and can afford electricity join the mining venture. By keeping those that are already supporting the Ethereum blockchain, stakeholders are invested in validating transactions in a conscientious way. After all, it is their economy that they are trying to build.

Dapps and the Participation of the People

How will the Ether get spread around if no one really gets an incentive for mining? The most logical answer for this is involving people in dapp projects. Right now, most of the dapps are in the beta stage, wherein their developers are encouraging people to join them, in exchange of tokens or Ether. Developers are also able to spread around Ether and app coins as payment for transactions that they do with other developers or dapp users.

App tokens are very interesting because it allows several Ethereum projects to get launched and become maintained without even having to rely on any venture capitalist. Some dapps that have gone live now were able to raise more than $250 million by simply creating app tokens which has the following characteristics

1. Tokens are the currencies that can be used within the app where they are created. You can think of them as the gold coins that you earn in a computer gam which, of course, can only be spent within the game. However, if you need more access, you can actually purchase them using fiat currency or another cryptocurrency that has value.

2. Everyone that contributes to the growth of the app is compensated by tokens. That means that when you contribute, you gain more access to the features of the app or get more tokens.

3. Tokens work like other cryptocurrencies – the more people are likely to use it, the more expensive they get. Moreover, you can convert them to any currency, depending on the value ascribed to it.

One classic example of a dapp that has made it big thanks to its own coins is Stork, which is a file storage application. There is no central figure that operates it and runs solely on the blockchain network that power. The Storjcoin is created as the application's currency that allows its users to buy storage space.

What makes app tokens lucrative in a sense is that you can actually hold on to them until they go up in value, then convert them into a different currency of your choice.

This brings up a whole new dimension when it comes to making money in the world of blockchains. Creators of dapps are incentivized when their creations become a success, and people that are already supporting them get a share of wealth by trading the coins that they already have. This creates a win-win scenario in the dapp scene, since this will inspire other developers to invest in another developer's creation and also create an application that will be very useful to the community in order to get the support that they want in order to succeed. Since this business model creates an atmosphere that is very independent, every developer has a chance of actually creating a successful project even if they have limited budget.

Chapter 9

Beginners Guide to Investing in Cryptocurrency

Having read the previous chapter, you might be thinking that you want to have a time machine and travel back to 2011 when Bitcoin seems like a shrouded experiment that is very cheap to invest in. However, investing in cryptocurrencies is definitely not for the faint of heart – it takes certain knowledge in order to make a smart investment.

Why Invest, and Why You Shouldn't

Besides what you have read so far, there are only three reasons why it is wise to invest in any form of cryptocurrency:

1. You want to protect yourself from the fall of the Dollar, which people assume to happen at some point in time

2. You actually support the goals that lead the cryptocurrency to what it aims to create, which is a free world that enjoys a free market

3. You understand what blockchains are and you actually like technology.

However, you need to keep in mind that there are also some bad reasons that you may already be thinking of (and are influencing you) when it comes to investing in a virtual currency. First, if you think that you are just falling to the hype of making quick money with this, then stop. If there is something that is telling you that you want to spend all your resources to buy cryptocurrency while you can still afford it, then you may be better off doing something else. Keep in mind that you should always learn what you are getting into before you even spend a dollar in a currency that you will not be able to touch.

One of the things that you need to remember is that cryptocurrencies function in order to support the goals of the blockchains that they operate in. More than just having a value in your currency, you may want to invest in them simply because you will need them to take advantage of what their blockchain's technology has to offer.

How are You Going to Get Them?

The easiest way to get cryptocurrency is to buy them. If you are interested in buying a Bitcoin, for example, you can go to an exchange site such as coinbase.com and use their online wallet to store your purchase. Another site that you may want to check out is the coinmarketcap.com

You can also opt to mine the currencies by participating on the blockchain network that is running thecryptocurrency that you are eyeing. Mining would involve having to spend on hardware and electricity in order to confirm transactions, but this can become a very lucrative source of passive income once you have everything set up and running. However, you can only do this on cryptocurrencies that are powered by the Proof of Work system.

You can also grow your digital money by doing staking, which is essentially the Proof of Stake version of mining. You may get different rewards by doing this, but it would need less physical investment compared to mining using hardware and electricity.

Another method of getting cryptocurrency in your wallet is to do arbitraging. Arbitraging is essentially the buy-and-sell method of acquiring and selling cryptocurrencies that you can get your hands on in order to get cash out of them and to grow your portfolio as well.

Review the Alternative Currencies

In early 2016, the Bitcoin practically has the entire cryptomarket for itself. However, that is not the case now, as you have read in the previous chapter. Nevertheless, there are hundreds of other cryptocurrencies out there, and you may want to invest in those that actually cater to how you want to spend them, and not just their current worth.

How would you know whether a cryptocurrency is worth investing in? There are three main factors that you need to consider:

1. The currency's trading volume and its market capitalization

Market capitalization refers to the amount of value ascribed to all the coins of the cryptocurrency available in circulation. When the market capitalization of the cryptocurrency you're eyeing is high, that can mean two things: it's either people are really putting value to the currency or there's a lot of it available in all markets that it is participating in. For this reason, you will also need to pay attention to its daily trading volume. If the trading volume is high on a daily basis, then it means that it is widely used in transactions, which is an indication of a healthy economy.

2. The currency's verification method

The verification method is the one that would really set cryptocurrencies apart. As explained earlier, the verification method is the process wherein a blockchain system agrees on whether a transaction is valid or not, and is also the way the cryptocurrency is generated and spread among members of the network.

3. Acceptance

Just like fiat currency, a cryptocurrency doesn't have any use if other people are not willing to buy it from you or if you cannot exchange it for any goods or services. For this reason, it is always best to invest in cryptocurrencies that has a healthy market that is welcome to use it for an exchange.

With these things in mind, you may want to ask yourself the following questions:

1. Do you think that your investment is safe with the development team?

   Time to remind yourself of the first rule of investing: always make sure that your capital is preserved. At this point, you may want to do some research when you are going to buy a currency or store your virtual money in your wallet. Do you want to leave your hard-earned money with a development team that has been hacked in the past? Did you read that they were involved in a scam? While the coin that they are offering might grow in the future, you may want to think twice before investing with them.

2. Does the currency that you want to invest in has a long-term plan?

   Again, more than being exchanged into cash, you may want to think about what the currency is trying to achieve in the first place. Most cryptocurrencies disclose their white paper, and if you have not read it yet, then it's high time that you do so. Is this cryptocurrency capable of achieving their project goals? What would the project that they have in mind look like in 10 years? Asking yourself this question will help you recognize a cryptocurrency that will grow in value.

If you think that the cryptocurrency that you're eyeing is just great at marketing but has no backup plan when things don't go their way, then you might just be investing in an ICO that has a great website but is not capable of delivering.

3. How long are you going to stay with the currency?

If you are after monetary gain, it pays to know which coins will be great to flip in order for you to enjoy their short-term benefits. When you acquire a currency or plan to do so, set your personal expectations and your exit price.

To read more about Cryptocurrency order my other book now available.

Cryptocurrency - Learn Cryptocurrency Technology Quickly

What you need to know in an hour

Chapter 10:

The Future of Blockchain

Blockchain is predicted to be as massive as the internet now – it is predicted to take over most, if not all, of the transactions that you are capable of doing now. Moreover, it will change the way you think about data and security.

At this point, people are just beginning to see what blockchain can actually do, thanks to current innovations that have gone live. However, think of it as the internet in the 1980s – back then, the concept of World Wide Web is intimidating, and transactions are infuriatingly slow. However, people were quick to see that it would revolutionize two aspects of the human condition: communication and education. In the end, it boils down to letting people access what they normally cannot in the status quo.

Blockchain achieves to do the same in different ways – in about ten years, this technology will change institutions, starting from the goal of freeing consumers from third parties that mediate exchanges. This goal, in itself, already changes a lot of things.

Apart from people actually having direct access to information, they will also have a free hand over creating and expressing themselves. This immediately disrupts a number of processes that people do in their daily lives. With the possibility of dapps, people can be as innovative as they can get within a blockchain's system. Internet is also unlikely to be regulated anymore. Because there is no single point of failure, blockchains predict a future where no task is left undone.

It does not mean though that all blockchains are perfect. It pays to always remember that they are designed to rigidly store the information that has already been approved by its network. While decentralizing decision making may be ideal in so many levels, there are also circumstances in history wherein the majority could be wrong. At the same time, it also does not mean that the majority can not be manipulated.

However, it pays to understand that the blockchain that you may know now is arguably not the blockchain that you will know tomorrow. It is possible that the Bitcoin will not be the largest cryptocurrency in the market and could be replaced by an unknown alt coin that you may not be even aware of today. It is possible that this technology may even prove to be negatively deconstructive in certain industries. After all, the blockchain is as only good as the program that it is built on, and the success of every platform built on this technology would depend on its participants.

Right now, there are too many speculations about the impact of the blockchain – it might sound too good to be true, but this might be the utopia that people are clamoring for, thanks to its ability to give power to multiple persons to make decisions and have control over its functions. However, this also means that responsibility and accountability is also dispersed to many different levels in a network. At this point, people may argue that individuals may not be ready for this kind of personal responsibility and freedom.

The Takeaway

In the end, the blockchain lies on the people's ability to take control of their future without having to rely on systems that may exist today. Just like any large innovation, the blockchain provides people a more direct access to their needs, allowing them to be more empowered in creating technologies that will make personal development possible.

However, the blockchain is still a work in progress – its process and its ability to fulfill the promise of being independent and free from manipulation is still under development. At this point, you and the other people who already know a thing or two about this emerging technology are its beta testers that are likely to encounter bugs while it is being slowly rolled out.

But this does not mean that the blockchain will fail at what it promises to do – the more you involve yourself with projects that already use it, the more insight you will have on how things could actually turn out in the future. If you want the blockchain to succeed and deliver, you will need to be part of its development team today.

Conclusion

Thank you for reading this book!

I hope this book helped you understand what the blockchain technology is and how this technology will change your life in the very near future. I also hope that you were able to grasp its importance and how you can apply its principles and current developments in your daily life.

Now, here is a challenge for you: go online and explore applications in your industry that has already gone live. Now is the perfect time for you to participate in the blockchain development and contribute to how it can be improved.

One more thing: could I ask you a favor? If you enjoyed this book as much as I enjoyed writing it, would you be so kind to leave your rating and your thoughts at Amazon.com? It would really help me create better books for you in the future.

Preview Of ' Cryptocurrency –Learn Cryptocurrency Quickly. What you need to know in an hour'

Definition

A cryptocurrency system relies on a key component called a blockchain, and these two terms have sometimes been used interchangeably. The blockchain, which we will be describing in detail in this chapter, is the underlying protocol that allows for the transfer of cryptocurrency and ensures a bulletproof transaction verification system to avoid fraud and malice. It is the most significant and powerful development in cryptocurrency technology. The power of this technology also lies in its capability in distributing information across all the individual computers (called nodes) within the system. The term blockchain has often been interchanged with distributed ledger technology.

The advantage of blockchain is it is distributed across all the nodes in the system. A particular cryptocurrency's blockchain database does not exist in a single location or is under the control of a single central authority, but exists or is hosted by thousands of computers at any single time.

The blockchain network contains a self-review or auditing system that because of the thousands of users confirming transactions, practically guarantee the accuracy and integrity of transactions and data residing in its ledgers. This security feature of a blockchain system is mostly brought about by the cryptographic manipulation and verification of data making it mathematically improbable to manipulate, change, and duplicate transactions. Not even massive computer power can hope to disrupt the blockchain system.

Blockchains are composed of three core parts:

The Block: This is simply transactions that are listed in a ledger over time. The amount, the time period, the number of transactions, and the even that triggered the creation of the block (payment, transfer, receipt) is different for each block. It would look like the following, non-digitally:

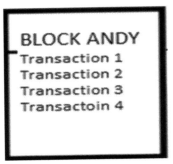

BLOCK ANDY
Transaction 1
Transaction 2
Transaction 3
Transactoin 4

Chain: Every block contains a hash of the previous block that "chained" it to the previous one. A computed hash successfully computed by a node mathematically links the block to another block. This concept is one of the most complex and difficult ones to understand in the cryptocurrency system, because it requires the use of fairly advanced arithmetic. But the chain is the glue magic that links the blocks together and provides the system of mathematical "trust" where no other trust exists in the cryptographic universe.

To read the rest of this book order now

Cryptocurrency - Learn Cryptocurrency Technology Quickly

What you need to know in an hour

Made in the USA
Middletown, DE
12 November 2017